Marc Martin is an award-winning illustrator based in Melbourne,
Australia. Working in a variety of mediums, Marc's work is a
world of dense colour, rich textures and the odd scribble.
More of his artwork can be found at www.marcmartin.com

BIG PICTURE PRESS
www.bigpicturepress.net

First published in the UK in 2015 by Big Picture Press,
an imprint of Bonnier Publishing Limited,
Deepdene Lodge, Deepdene Avenue, Dorking, Surrey, RH5 4AT, UK
www.templarco.co.uk

First published by Penguin Group (Australia) 2013

ISBN 978-1-78370-194-0

Printed in Malaysia

Designed by Marc Martin and Amanda Newman/Perfect Bound Ltd

The Curious Explorer's Illustrated Guide to

EXOTIC ANIMALS

A TO Z

by Marc Martin

Armadillo *Dasypus novemcinctus*

Bird of Paradise *Lophorina superba*

C   Chameleon   *Trioceros jacksonii*

Dodo *Raphus cucullatus*

E Electric Eel *Electrophorus electricus*

Flamingo *Phoenicopterus ruber*

F

G Galápagos Giant Tortoise *Chelonoidis nigra*

Hippopotamus *Hippopotamus amphibius*

I Ibex *Capra sibirica*

Jellyfish *Medusozoa*

J

K Kangaroo *Macropus rufus*

Loris *Loris tardigradus*

L

M Macaw *Ara ararauna, Ara militaris, Ara macao*

N Narwhal *Monodon monoceros*

Owl *Tyto multipunctata*

Panda *Ailuropoda melanoleuca*

Quetzal *Pharomachrus mocinno*

Q

R Redback Spider *Latrodectus hasselti*

Sea Dragon *Phycodurus eques*

S

T Tasmanian Devil *Sarcophilus harrisii*

Ulysses Butterfly *Papilio ulysses*

U

V Vampire Bat *Desmodus rotundus*

Walrus *Odobenus rosmarus*

W

X-ray Fish *Pristella maxillaris*

Yellow-tailed Black Cockatoo
Calyptorhynchus funereus

Y

Z Zebra *Equus zebra*

Armadillo means 'little armoured one' in Spanish and describes the bony plates that cover the mammal's body. The nine-banded armadillo (*Dasypus novemcinctus*) inhabits parts of the United States, and Central and South America. Armadillos can hold their breath for six minutes, which helps them to dig for worms and grubs without inhaling dirt.

Birds of Paradise are known for their beautiful feathers. The Superb Bird of Paradise (*Lophorina superba*) lives in rainforests throughout the island of New Guinea. The male performs an unusual dance to attract female birds, spreading his front feathers into a large blue oval, snapping his tail feathers loudly together and hopping in circles around the female.

Chameleons are very colourful lizards. The Jackson's Chameleon (*Trioceros jacksonii*) is native to the humid, cooler regions of Kenya and Tanzania. It is sometimes called the Three-horned Chameleon because males of the species have three horns: one on the nose and one above each eye. Chameleons change colour according to their mood. For example, some chameleons will change from green to red and yellow when they are angry.

Dodos (*Raphus cucullatus*) are extinct flightless birds that once lived on the island of Mauritius. The dodo became extinct in the late 1600s due to habitat destruction, introduced predators and hunting. No complete dodo specimens exist today, and its appearance is only recorded in paintings and written accounts from the 17th century.

Electric Eels (*Electrophorus electricus*) are found in the fresh waters of the Amazon and Orinoco River basins of South America. Despite the electric eel's name, it is not actually an eel but a fish. Its body contains electric organs with about 6,000 cells called electrocytes that store power like small batteries and allow it to stun predators and prey.

Flamingos are found in parts of Africa, Southern Asia, Southern Europe, the Caribbean, and Central and South America. The American Flamingo (*Phoenicopterus ruber*) is often seen standing on one leg, which is thought to allow it to conserve body heat, as it spends significant amounts of time wading in cold water.

Galápagos Giant Tortoises (*Chelonoidis nigra*) live on the Galápagos islands, west of mainland Ecuador. They are the longest-living of all vertebrates, with an average life span of over 100 years. Galápagos tortoises have a very slow metabolism, sleeping nearly 16 hours a day, and can survive up to a year without eating or drinking.

Hippopotamuses (*Hippopotamus amphibius*) live in sub-Saharan Africa. The word 'hippopotamus' is from ancient Greek, meaning 'river horse'. Hippopotamuses love water, and have webbed toes to help them paddle. When basking on the shore, their skin produces an oily substance which acts as a natural skin moistener and sunscreen.

Ibex are very good climbers, and can climb up and down steep cliffs with ease. The Siberian Ibex (*Capra sibirica*) lives in alpine meadows in central and northern Asia. Adult ibex give off a loud whistle when in danger, and their ability to move nimbly on steep, rocky terrain helps them avoid predators such as wolves, snow leopards and brown bears.

Jellyfish (*Medusozoa*) are found in every ocean around the world, with some jellyfish also inhabiting fresh water. They usually live in large groups, called blooms, and have wandered the oceans for at least 500 million years. Made up of 95 per cent water, jellyfish propel themselves using their bell-shaped bodies, and catch food (such as fish and zooplankton) with their stinging tentacles.

Kangaroos are found across mainland Australia. The Red Kangaroo (*Macropus rufus*) is the largest of all kangaroos, standing approximately 1.5 metres (5 feet) tall and weighing up to 90 kilograms (200 pounds). A red kangaroo can reach speeds of 50 kilometres (30 miles) an hour, and can jump distances of up to 8 metres (26 feet) in length and almost 2 metres (6½ feet) in height.

Lorises are found in tropical and woodland forests in India, Sri Lanka, and other parts of South-East Asia. The Slender Loris (*Loris tardigradus*) is a slow-moving, nocturnal primate. It is a very good climber, and can hang from branches using only its feet. If feeling threatened, the loris will sometimes bite its predators with venom stored in a gland in its arm, which it licks and mixes with saliva.

Macaws are native to Mexico, Central America, and South America. Blue-and-yellow Macaws (*Ara ararauna*), Military Macaws (*Ara militaris*) and Scarlet Macaws (*Ara macao*) are just three of 17 species of macaw. They are zygodactyl birds, which means that their first and fourth toes point backwards.

Narwhals (*Monodon monoceros*) live in the Arctic waters around Canada and Greenland. Sometimes called the unicorn of the sea, the male Narwhal has a prominent tooth that grows into a spiral tusk up to 2.7 metres (9 feet) long. Narwhals are also very good divers, plunging to depths of up to 1.5 kilometres (1 mile) below the surface.

Owls are mostly solitary, nocturnal birds. The Lesser Sooty Owl (*Tyto multipunctata*) is a species of owl that lives in the wet tropics region of Australia. An owl has three eyelids: one for blinking, one for sleeping and one for cleaning the eye.

Pandas (*Ailuropoda melanoleuca*) are found in central-western and south-western China. They eat mostly bamboo and sometimes birds or rodents as well. A typical giant panda will spend about 12 out of every 24 hours eating. They are also very good tree-climbers and swimmers.

Quetzals are mostly solitary birds that feed on fruits, berries, insects and small animals. The Resplendent Quetzal (*Pharomachrus mocinno*) is found in the mountainous, tropical forests of Central America. Male quetzals' tail feathers can grow up to an incredible 1 metre (3 feet 3 inches) long during mating season.

Redback Spiders (*Latrodectus hasselti*) are found throughout Australia. Redbacks (as they are commonly known) are considered one of the most dangerous species of spider in Australia. Only the female carries the distinguishing red stripe the spider is known for – the male is light brown in colour with white markings on its back.

Sea Dragons are found along the southern and western coasts of Australia. The Leafy Sea Dragon (*Phycodurus eques*) uses small, transparent fins to propel and steer itself through the water, and is covered with leaf-shaped appendages that serve as camouflage and give the Sea Dragon the appearance of floating seaweed.

Tasmanian Devils (*Sarcophilus harrisii*) are found on the Australian island of Tasmania, south of the mainland. They are notoriously bad-tempered and make an extremely loud screech when disturbed. Sometimes before a fight, a Tasmanian Devil will use a sharp sneeze to challenge other devils.

Ulysses Butterflies (*Papilio ulysses*) are found in north-eastern Australia, New Guinea, and parts of Indonesia and the Solomon Islands. The male butterflies are strongly attracted to the colour blue, and sometimes mistake blue objects for female butterflies.

Vampire Bats (*Desmodus rotundus*) are found in the tropics of Mexico, Central America, and South America. They feed on blood from sleeping cows, pigs, horses and birds, but rarely harm their prey. Vampire bats are clean animals and often groom themselves and the other bats in their group.

Walruses (*Odobenus rosmarus*) are found around the North Pole in the Arctic Ocean and sub-Arctic seas of the Northern Hemisphere. They have very bad eyesight, but their hearing and sense of smell are excellent. The walrus's whiskers are not hairs but sensitive organs that help them find food.

X-Ray Fish (*Pristella maxillaris*) are found in the coastal rivers of Brazil, French Guiana, Guyana and Venezuela. A translucent layer of skin covers their bodies and offers protection from predators who find it difficult to see them.

Yellow-tailed Black Cockatoos (*Calyptorhynchus funereus*) are native to south-east Australia. They can be extremely noisy, and their high-pitched calls can be heard from far away. Like all birds, they have hollow bones that make them very light and able to fly – often very acrobatically. Cockatoos can live to be more than 50 years old.

Zebras have stripes that cover their bodies and act as camouflage. The Mountain Zebra (*Equus zebra*) is a threatened species of zebra native to south-western Angola, Namibia and South Africa. The zebra's stripes make a herd of zebra on the move confusing to predators. Like fingerprints, no two sets of zebra stripes are exactly the same.

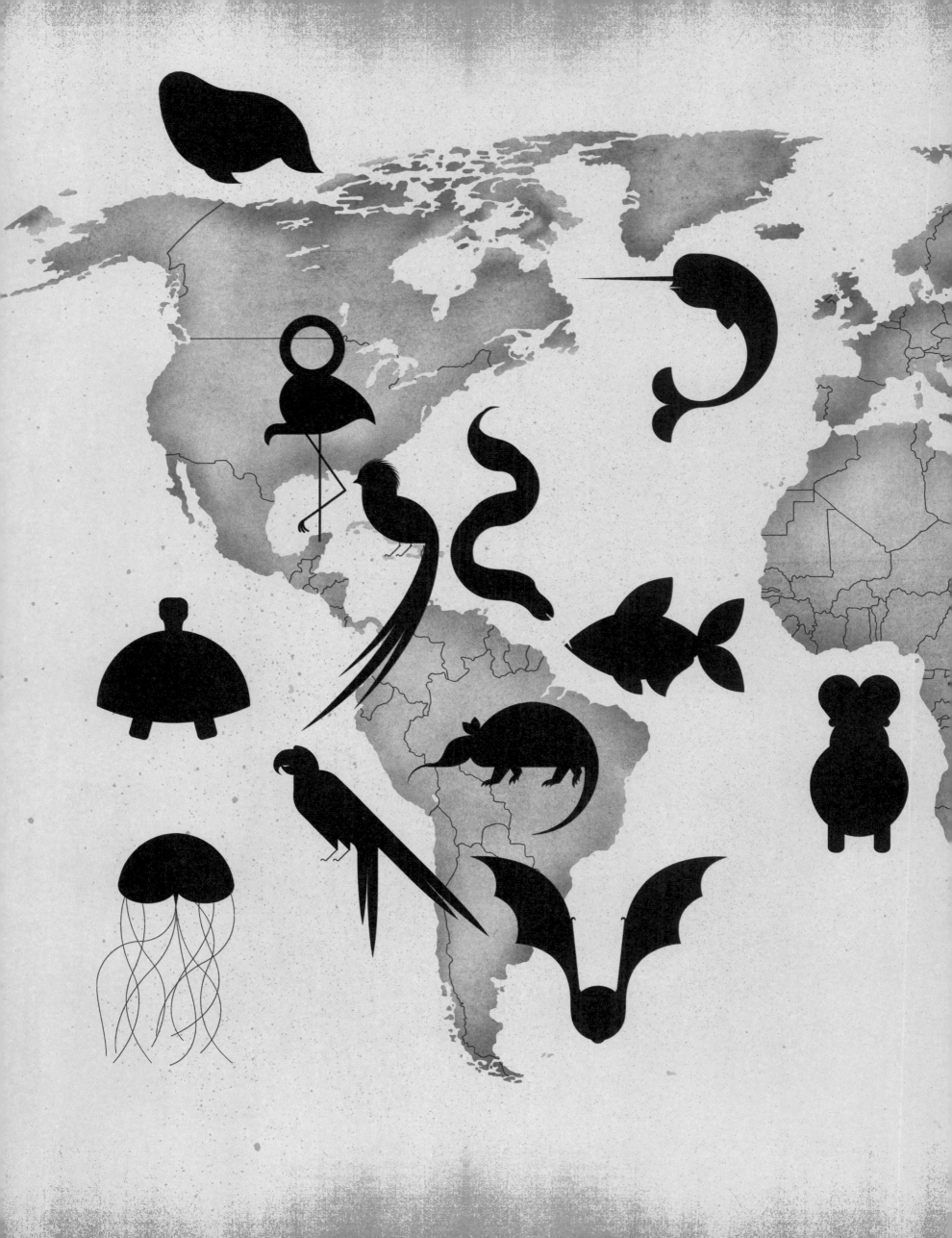